Ravens

Emma Carlson Berne

D1283545

PowerKiDS press™

New York

Published in 2015 by The Rosen Publishing Group, Inc.
29 East 21st Street, New York, NY 10010

First Edition

Editor: Joanne Randolph
Book Design: Joe Carney
Photo Research: Katie Stryker

Photo Credits: Cover James Hager/Robert Harding World Imagery/Getty Images; p. 5 MSMcCarthy_Photography/iStock/Thinkstock.com; p. 7 (top/bottom) Visuals Unlimited, Inc./Fabio Pupin/Getty Images; p. 8 Anna Kucherova/iStock/Thinkstock; p. 9 altrendo nature/Getty Images; p. 10 Klaus Nigge/National Geographic/Getty Images; p. 11 creepers888/iStock/Thinkstock; p. 12 fototip/Shutterstock.com; p. 13 ???iana Makotra/Hemera/Thinkstock.com; p. 15 Robbie George/National Geographic/Getty Images; p. 16 Mati Kurg/iStock/Thinkstock; p. 17 Ken Hoehn/iStock/Thinkstock; p. 19 Stephen Meese/iStock/Thinkstock; p. 20 Michael S. Quinton/National Geographic/Getty Images; p. 21 © Ardea/Zipp, Jim/Animals Animals; p. 22 bgsmith/iStock/Thinkstock.

Library of Congress Cataloging-in-Publication Data

Berne, Emma Carlson, author.
 Ravens / by Emma Carlson Berne. — 1st ed.
     pages cm. — (Scavengers, eating nature's trash)
 Includes index.
 ISBN 978-1-4777-6612-5 (library binding) — ISBN 978-1-4777-6613-2 (pbk.) —
ISBN 978-1-4777-6614-9 (6-pack)
 1. Ravens—Juvenile literature. 2. Scavengers (Zoology)—Juvenile literature. 3. Ecology—Juvenile literature. I. Title.
 QL696.P2367B37 2015
 598.8'64—dc23
                                              2014000514

Manufactured in the United States of America

CPSIA Compliance Information: Batch #WS14PK6: For Further Information contact Rosen Publishing, New York, New York at 1-800-237-9932

Contents

Remarkable Ravens

Picture a big, glossy black bird soaring high in the air. This is the raven, which is the largest **passerine** bird. A passerine bird is one that has feet that allow it to perch on branches.

Ravens are hunters, **foragers**, and **scavengers**. They plan ahead to get food and think of clever solutions to problems. Some people think they are as smart as dogs.

Ravens have fascinated people for a long time. A famous poet named Edgar Allan Poe even wrote a long poem about a raven that haunts a man. Many other groups of people have told stories about this intelligent, **adaptable** bird.

The largest bird in the crow family, ravens have large bills, which they use to eat dead animals, hunt for living ones, and to dig into human garbage.

All About Ravens

Ravens live all through the northern and western United States. They live in Canada and Alaska and down into Mexico. They live throughout Europe, Africa, and parts of Asia, too.

KEY
Common raven range

This map shows the parts of the world in which common ravens live.

The raven most of us know is the common raven. Its scientific name is *Corvus corax*. Ravens are related to crows and jays. Adult common ravens are all black with black feet and eyes. Some **subspecies** of ravens have some dark brown feathers on their bodies. Others have white feathers on their necks. The thick-billed raven, which lives in northeast Africa, has a heavy beak that takes up most of its face, much like a toucan's.

The white-necked raven lives in southern Africa. These birds are smaller than common ravens but have larger bills.

These brown-necked ravens live in Yemen, which sits on the southern coast of the Arabian Peninsula. This species of raven lives throughout northern Africa into the Middle East.

An Adaptable Bird

Like many scavengers, ravens can live in all sorts of different **habitats**. They can live out on the plains, or open grasslands, in forests, on cliffs over the sea, in cities near landfills and dumps, in suburbs, high on mountains, or in the desert. Ravens can live in all these places because they are adaptable. This means they can change how they live to fit their surroundings. They can eat all sorts of different foods and make their nests out of many different materials.

Ravens are more than happy living in cities and towns near people. Animals that are able to do this are much better off than animals that cannot since people keep taking over natural habitats to build homes and businesses.

This raven is eating garbage from trash cans in the mountainside park where it lives.

More and More Ravens

For years, people hunted and trapped ravens because farmers thought they killed livestock. That practice has mostly stopped, and the raven population is expanding once more.

One Smart Bird

Ravens are very smart. Scientists have studied ravens and found that they plan and solve problems. Ravens have been known to make traps for other animals and put bait in them. When an animal shows up to eat what it thinks is an easy snack, the raven is ready. Ravens also stack or pile food in unusual ways in order to carry it away more easily.

In order to be able to carry away eggs, ravens peck into the shell and grab the leg of the chick inside.

Ravens have been known to wait in trees near a sheep that is about to give birth. Once the lamb is born, the raven swoops in and grabs it.

Ravens will also work together to hunt or forage. Ravens love eggs. Often one raven will distract a female bird, while the other raven steals the egg out from under her in the nest. In the Arctic, one raven will peck a young seal to death, while another one keeps the seal from getting away. Then they both share in the kill.

Ravens Eat Anything

Like pigs, coyotes, bears, and humans, ravens are **omnivores**. They can eat an amazing variety of food. This includes live rodents and small mammals, roadkill and **carcasses**, corn, acorns, eggs, clams and mussels, dead fish, seeds and fruit of all kinds, insects, and earthworms. Ravens will also eat human garbage. You can sometimes see them flying in circles around landfills, trying to catch a glimpse of a tasty treat.

Ravens will eat seeds, nuts, fruit, grains, and berries. They generally eat whatever they can find, which is why they are so successful.

This raven has found a piece of meat in someone's garbage.

Ravens usually perch on the ground to eat and hold food down with their feet. Sometimes they will carry off extra food and hide it in a safe place for later.

A Scavenger, Too

There are lots of ravens in the world. One reason the raven population has survived is that they are very good scavengers.

They can eat an amazing variety of human food scraps and often scour dumps for garbage. You may see a raven perched at the roadside, picking with its strong beak at a dead animal that has been hit by a car.

A Wolf Helper

Ravens sometimes get animals to help them get food they want. For instance, ravens can't tear apart an animal carcass, but wolves can. Ravens will fly ahead of the wolves to lead them to **prey**. They then wait patiently for the wolves' leftovers.

This raven has found a dead deer to eat.

Social Birds

Ravens are social, playful birds. They are wild animals, but some people have tamed ravens and found that they are friendly pets that like being with people. Sometimes, ravens will amuse themselves by teasing other animals, such as dogs or cats.

Generally large groups of ravens together are likely to be young ravens that have not paired up yet.

Most often ravens are seen in pairs, such as this one.

Ravens **mate** for life. Mates often play together, pulling each other's tails or passing stones to each other. They also like to fly with sticks, which they drop and try to catch in midair. Pairs rest and sleep together, too. Sometimes they come together in large flocks of more than 100 birds. Unlike their cousins the crows, though, ravens spend more time alone or in pairs.

A Lot to Say

Ravens are some of the most intelligent birds. Like parrots, another very smart bird, ravens are good mimics. They can copy the calls of other birds. People who own tame ravens report that the birds can be taught to repeat words, too.

Ravens also make many different calls to each other. Some calls are meant to keep other ravens out of their territories. Others are alarm calls used when their nests are disturbed. Scientists have divided raven calls into 33 different categories of meaning.

Acrobats!

Ravens are excellent, acrobatic fliers. They can do somersaults in midair, tumble, free-fall, even glide upside down in a corkscrew pattern. One bird was spotted flying upside down for .5 mile (805 m). Young ravens will sometimes play games with sticks, flying with them, dropping them out of their claws, and then diving to catch them in midair.

Their ability to mimic other birds' calls may help them sneak up on nests to steal eggs and hatchlings.

In a Raven's Nest

After a male and female raven mate, the pair builds a nest high up in a tree, on a telephone pole, or even on the ledge of a skyscraper. They stack sticks to make the outside and then line the inside with mud. Then they pad the inside of the mud cup with soft material that they find. This might include wool, grass, feathers, hair, and rags.

As with other birds, ravens swallow the food they catch to break it down before bringing it back up and putting it inside their babies' mouths.

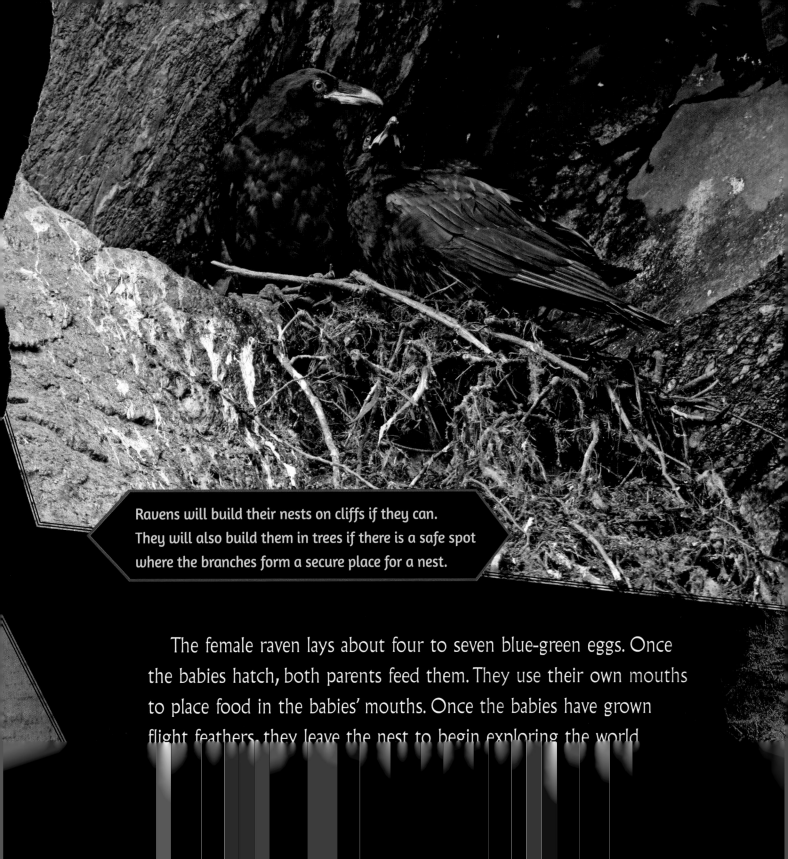

Ravens will build their nests on cliffs if they can.
They will also build them in trees if there is a safe spot
where the branches form a secure place for a nest.

The female raven lays about four to seven blue-green eggs. Once the babies hatch, both parents feed them. They use their own mouths to place food in the babies' mouths. Once the babies have grown flight feathers, they leave the nest to begin exploring the world

A Bird with Many Stories

People have always noticed ravens and told stories about them. Some people thought that they were **omens** of death, maybe because of their black color.

Many Native American tribes have told legends about Raven. They often describe him as a smart, tricky character who can turn himself into other animals. No matter what stories are told, these big, beautiful birds are unique and wonderful members of our ecosystem.

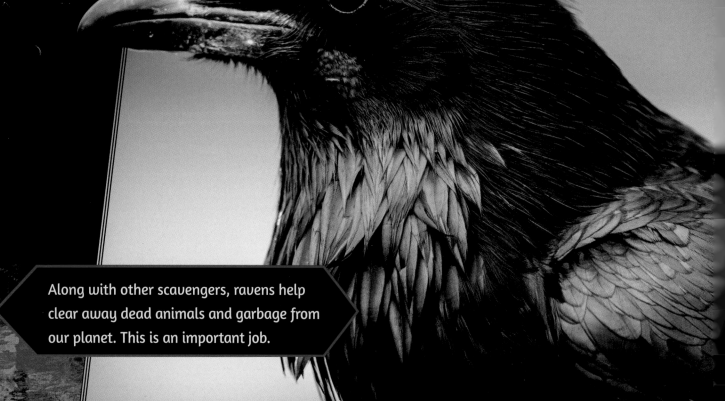

Along with other scavengers, ravens help clear away dead animals and garbage from our planet. This is an important job.

Glossary

adaptable (uh-DAPT-uh-bul) Able to change to fit new conditions.

carcasses (KAR-kus-ez) Dead bodies.

foragers (FOR-ij-erz) People or animals that hunt or search for food.

habitats (HA-buh-tats) The kinds of land where animals or plants naturally live.

mate (MAYT) To be a pair for making babies.

omens (OH-menz) Things, like objects or animals, that are believed to be warnings or signs of future events.

omnivores (OM-nih-vorz) Animals that eat both plants and animals.

passerine (PA-seh-ryn) Having to do with a group of birds, which includes almost half of all bird species, that have feet that can perch on branches.

scavengers (SKA-ven-jurz) Animals that eat dead things.

subspecies (SUB-spee-sheez) Animals in the same species or group that look slightly different and live in different places.

Index

A
Africa, 6–7

B
beak, 7, 14

C
carcass(es), 12, 14
crows, 7, 17

F
feathers, 7, 20–21
feet, 4, 7, 13
food(s), 4, 8, 10, 12–14, 21

G
grasslands, 8

H
habitats, 8
hunters, 4

J
jays, 7

M
Mexico, 6

N
name, 7

O
omens, 22
omnivores, 12

P
plains, 8
Poe, Edgar Allan, 4
problems, 4, 10

S
subspecies, 7

U
United States, 6

Websites

Due to the changing nature of Internet links, PowerKids Press has developed an online list of websites related to the subject of this book. This site is updated regularly. Please use this link to access the list:
www.powerkidslinks.com/scav/raven/